THE ILLUSTRATED HISTORY OF

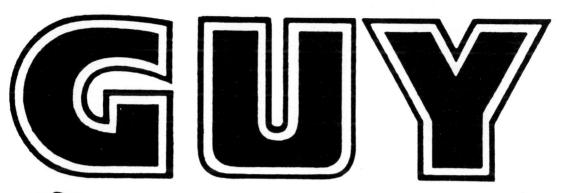

GUY

TRUCKS & BUSES

THE ILLUSTRATED HISTORY OF

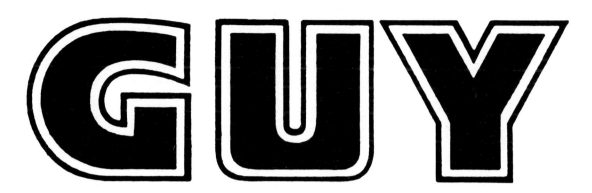

GUY

TRUCKS & BUSES

ANTHONY E. GUY

A **FOULIS** Motoring Book

First published 1989
© Anthony E. Guy 1989

Published by:
Haynes Publishing Group
Sparkford, Nr. Yeovil, Somerset. BA22 7JJ. England

Haynes Publications Inc.
861 Lawrence Drive, Newbury Park, California
91320 USA

British Library Cataloguing in Publication Data
Guy, A.E.
    The illustrated history of Guy trucks & buses.
    1. Guy commercial vehicles to 1988
    I. Title
    629.2'24

ISBN 0-85429-719-7

Library of Congress Catalog Card Number
88-83696

Editor: Robert Iles
Page Layout: Peter Kay
Printed in England by:
J.H. Haynes & Co. Ltd.

Acknowledgements

Thanks are due to *Commercial Motor* and *Old Motor* magazines (relaunched as *Classic and Sportscar)*, Robin Hannay, the Omnibus Society and Jaguar Cars Ltd, for their co-operation and assistance during the writing of this book.

Foreword

The history of industry is rich with stories of the activities of leading personalities, and their achievements or failures are reflected in the march of progress. The improvement of road transport during the first half of this century greatly affected the industrial and social life of the country, and is typically exemplified in the history of Guy Motors Ltd. over this period.

Sydney S. Guy gained his practical engineering experience with the Belliss and Morcom Steam Engineering Company, the General Electric Company and the Humber Company of Coventry during the early days of the motor car. Later he joined the old Sunbeam Motor Company of Wolverhampton, where he was Works Manager at the time when Louis Coatalen was designing the brilliant race-winning Sunbeam cars.

At the end of 1913, Mr. Sydney S. Guy resigned from his position as Works Manager to the Sunbeam Motor Car Co. Ltd. and in May 1914, with the backing of some good friends, launched his own company, Guy Motors Ltd. Up to the time of his retirement in 1957, Sydney Guy developed and led his Wolverhampton organization with the enthusiasm and drive that has possessed all true pioneers of industry.

Tribute should also be paid to the many loyal members of the team which helped him to build up Guy Motors including, in particular, his brother, William Ewart Guy, whose great personality and determination contributed substantially to the marketing of the Company's products.

The factory was built at Fallings Park, Wolverhampton, in May 1914. Since that time, it was developed in order to cope with the increasing demands of road transport and the absorption of the Sunbeam Trolley Bus Co. in 1948. The buildings eventually covered an area of fourteen acres and some 2000 people were employed during World War II. Mr. Guy was always fully convinced that in any manufacturing organization employing more than that number, the personal touch tended to be lost, which was so necessary for harmonious working and for obtaining the highest possible degree of efficiency.

Mass production in its usually accepted sense was not attempted in the Guy concern as every vehicle was individually built for long life and low running costs. However, the works and plant was constantly kept up-to-date and equipped with the very latest machinery.

The story told in these pages is a succession of pioneering achievements to which, in good measure, can be traced the present-day efficiency of road transport. It will be seen that this record comprises distinct sections dealing with goods, military, passenger types, etc.

Pioneering Achievements

Most of the following designs and types originated by Guy Motors Ltd. have subsequently been adopted in various forms elsewhere.

1914	Overdrive and governed vehicle speed.
1914	Subframe mounted engine and gearbox.
1914	Light (2 ton) commercial vehicle.
1917	350 hp seven-cylinder radial aero-engine, produced in 24 days.
1918	12-cylinder aero-engine designed and built.
1919	$2^{1}/2$-3 ton battery electric vehicle.
1919	V8 engined car.
1919	Automatic chassis lubrication.
1920	'Spud' wheels for cross-country work.
1922	Promenade low loading runabout.
1923	Roadless (caterpillar track) type.
1924	Travelling showrooms.
1924	Low loading (drop frame) chassis.
1924	One-man operated bus, with patented emergency exit.
1925	First military six-wheel, four-wheel driven cross-country vehicle.
1926	Six-wheel, four-wheel driven double-deck petrol bus.
1926	Six-wheel, four-wheel driven electric double-deck trolley bus.
1926	Patented system of trolley bus regenerative control.
1927	Gas producer vehicle.
1928	Six-wheel, four-wheel driven armoured car.
1931	Six-wheel driven chassis.
1931	Eight-wheel driven chassis.
1937	Four-wheel driven QUAD ANT.
1938	Four-wheel driven LIZARD.
1939	Welding armoured plate bodies.
1940	First British rear-engined armoured car.
1941/5	Military vehicles and civilian versions thereof and ARAB double-deckers produced in large numbers to meet wartime needs.
1950	New look frontal treatment ARAB Mk. IV double-decker.
1952	Lightweight underfloor engined passenger chassis.
1957	Largest bus in the world. Rolls-Royce powered three-axle double-decker with 105 passenger capacity, supplied to Johannesburg Corporation.
1958	Most outstanding cab design ever to be seen on British commercial vehicles on INVINCIBLE and WARRIOR range.
1959	WILFRUNIAN double-decker bus with all-round air suspension and disc brakes. Well in advance of the times.
1960	VICTORY air suspension chassis introduced with raised flooring for underfloor luggage stowage. Highly successful model in export markets.

Feathers in our cap

The Original "Feathers in our Cap" advertisement showed a feather in the radiator cap for each important repeat order, and first appeared on 22nd January 1924. It was also reproduced as a full-size radiator shaped display board on the Guy Stand at the Commercial Vehicle Show at Olympia in the same year. The names appearing on each feather were Midland General Omnibus Co., War Office, Leeds Corporation, Keith & Boyle Ltd., Hull Corporation, Standard Motor Car Co., Harrods Ltd., W.A. Nightingale & Sons, Peak Frean & Co., Millward Ltd., Gas Light & Coke Co., H.E. Starling and Greenwich Seamans Hospital. During the Vehicle Show, it was suggested that the feathers should be formed into an Indian Warrior's full ceremonial head-dress. This proposal was adopted, and the Guy Indian Head mascot became one of the most famous symbols in the vehicle world.

The slogan "ten years in advance of the times" following in the next year, and was widely known throughout the world, together with "feathers in our cap".

Feathers in our cap advertisements (January 22nd 1924) and "10 years in advance of the times" showing easy removal of axle shafts.

The Guy V8 Car

Before World War I, Mr. Sydney Guy produced commercial vehicles bearing his name and after the Armistice, it became common knowledge in the trade that he was watching the running of his lorries with a view to producing a private car. Nothing more was heard of this project until the 1919 Show when the 20 hp Guy V-8 was announced, the prototype having been successfully kept secret during some 50,000 miles of testing, which had included a thirty-day consumption test in North Wales.

The Guy V8 had the distinction of being the first British V8 to go into production. Mr. E.D.J. Buckney, who was responsible for the design, although employing an eight-cylinder engine, nevertheless paid great attention to ease of maintenance in the hands of owner-drivers. The engine, of 72 by 125 mm, had two V-set banks of four cylinders and each bank had two detachable cylinder heads, so that it was only necessary to remove half a dozen nuts and a head to expose two pistons and four valves with the water connections, tappets and manifolding remaining undisturbed. Moreover, large hand-holes in the offside of the crankcase enabled the big-end bolts to be removed, and the pistons and rods could then be drawn up through the bores without disturbing the sump.

1919 Guy 8-cylinder car.

Details of the V8 engine

The valves lay side by side and the combustion chambers were so formed that the valve stems were horizontal, and all the valves could be operated by a single camshaft, set above the crankcase, between the cylinders. The camshaft was driven by a silent chain (with external means of adjustment) from the front of the crankshaft. A cross-shaft drove a B.L.I.C. magneto on the off side and a C.A.V. dynamo on the near side. There was one spark plug per cylinder in the head, with a compression tap beside it and the ignition leads were led neatly round the front and down each side of the engine in conduits. The crankcase was of light alloy, including the engine bearers and platforms for the components, and the base chamber and timing case were also of light alloy. The big-ends of each pair of connecting rods lay side by side on a common crankpin.

Cooling was by thermo-syphon with branch pipes leading to each cylinder head, the central exhaust manifold being water-cooled. A Zenith carburettor on each side fed into a heated pipe, inlet, exhaust and water outlet pipes, all being within the 'V' of the cylinder blocks. In spite of the close proximity of these pipes, the engine ran very cool and the Whittle fan belt could be removed in winter with advantage. From the camshaft a skew gear drive was taken to the oil pump in the centre of the sump, and all the oil was passed through a simple, but effective filter on the near side of the crankcase. The lid of this filter was stamped with the words "clean frequently", an operation which could be done very easily indeed.

A cone clutch, with its spigot lubricated from the engine, drove a four-speed gearbox in which every pinion was an individual unit for ease of replacement. Engine and gearbox were carried on a sub-frame, three-point suspended from the chassis on ball and socket mountings, and the right-hand gear lever was attached directly to the gearbox. An open shaft conveyed the drive to a spiral-bevel rear axle, so designed that it could be dismantled without jacking up the rear wheels. The chassis frame was conventional but had few cross-members, the three-point suspension of the power unit and the use of similar mountings for the radiator making considerable flexion a matter of little moment.

Suspension was by half-elliptic springs, underslung at the rear, devoid of dowels or drilled holes. It was claimed that the axles never went more than $1/32$ in. out of track, even over the roughest roads, as the camber of the rear springs was almost negatived when the car was fully loaded and the shackles were carefully laid out. Steering was by worm and wheel, the rake of the column being adjustable over a very wide arc and the wire wheels carried 820 by 120 mm tyres. The dash was a mixed cast-iron and light alloy structure carrying an aluminium instrument panel, and the speedometer was gearbox-driven.

Lubrication thoroughness

It was a proud claim for the Guy V8 that not a single grease cup was fitted. Excess engine oil fed the fan spindle and clutch spigot, excess gearbox oil supplied the front universal joint and the rear axle oil went to the rear universal, rear springs and wheel bearings. Oil cups were fed by wick to the steering connections, swivel pins and front-wheel bearings, and even the greaser on the dynamo was replaced by an oil cup. Nor was that all for a plunger pump, operated by the steering drop-arm every time full right-hand lock was used, supplied excess engine oil to the brake compensator, front springs, etc. An oil can was purposely omitted from the tool kit to emphasize the efficiency of this system.

The Guy V8 cost £1,275 as a chassis and some 140 to 150 cars were built before production ceased in 1925. Representative of a 'golden age' when cars were first designed and built, the price was then fixed and introduction to the sales department came subsequently. The Guy, not unnaturally, succumbed to later developments. Nevertheless, in its day, it was noted for a suspension system well able to cope with war-worn roads, a quiet engine and a brisk performance. In spite of its 10 ft. 10 in. wheelbase it constituted an economical, easily serviced car for owner-drivers.

Goods Vehicles

The first product of the Company was a 30 cwt. lorry in 1914 which incorporated some original ideas and was a definite advance on existing types. This vehicle was fitted with direct drive in third gear for use when fully laden, whilst the indirect top gear was used only when it was travelling 'light'. This same idea, in later years, was looked upon in some quarters as original, and known as 'overdrive'. The vehicle also had a governor fitted behind the gearbox which limited the road speed to 30 mph without affecting the engine speed on the indirect gears when hill climbing. Another novel feature was that the power unit was mounted on a three-point suspended sub-frame, thus preventing any distortion of the main frame from being transmitted to the engine or gearbox (see page 51). A modern development of this idea, called "floating power" or suspension, is incorporated in most makes of cars and commercial vehicles.

During World War I, the factory was virtually taken over for armament production, the Company thereby losing its commercial contacts. After the war, marketing difficulties were considerably increased owing to the thousands of surplus army lorries being thrown on the market by the Army Disposal Board.

In 1920, the Guy designers produced the first special vehicle for cross-country work. This was a farmer's lorry, having "spud" wheels which are in wide use on farm tractors to this day. Two years later, the Company built an articulated six-wheeler, and also produced a $2^1/2$-3 ton electric battery vehicle for refuse collection, along with a $2^1/2$-3 ton electric battery vehicle.

Road/rail vehicle

In 1923, there appeared a road/rail vehicle with twin engines, driving a single propeller shaft through a special gearbox. It was fitted with a bogie at the front for running on the rails and it had large rear driving wheels running outside the track and was used for hauling railway trucks. With the bogie uncoupled, it was equally at home on various types of roads.

Body building for various types of commercial uses had commenced and by 1924, the Company were supplying some of the most important operators in the country, many of whom continued to buy Guys from then on.

The particular batch of vehicles, of which this is an example, was produced for use in North Africa in connection with an uprising of the Moors.

1923 road/rail vehicle.

1920 2¹/₂ ton Guy vehicle of this type was exhibited at the first post-war Commercial Vehicle Show.

1921 An early farmer's vehicle with a movable upper deck.

1921 The makers of "The Best Car in the World" select a Guy.

1923 Another 'first' was the military vehicle produced in 1923. This was an army lorry which had pneumatic tyres and was built under Government contract.

1924 One of the early vehicles supplied to Harrods, who operated a large fleet of Guys.

1924 Tracked vehicles with "caterpillar" wheels were introduced. Whereas previously goods chassis were adapted for passenger applications, Guy now brought out the first dropped frame for buses and this development brought in orders from both home and overseas for large quantities of single deckers with "one-step" entry. Pneumatic tyres were also becoming universally accepted for goods and passenger vehicles.

1925 A gully emptier.

1925 One of the first travelling
showrooms.

1926 An early horse-box.

14

1926 In 1926 another
Wolverhampton firm was acquired
by Guy Motors, this being the Star
Motor Co., which had started life in
1899. Although Star cars, trucks and
buses continued to be produced
after this takeover, the range was
discontinued in 1932. All new car
spare parts were then sold to
Messrs. Mackenzie & Denly of Hall
Green, Birmingham, who continued
to build Star vehicles for two or
three years.

Guy Motors always prided itself on amicable relationships with employees. ''During the
General Strike of 1926'' says Sydney Guy, ''We found to our surprise that only a very few did
not work. When the strike was over, before our people were re-employed, we explained that
we did not care whether they belonged to a union or not, but felt it necessary to know''. The
Company formed a works committee which had proportional representation and, after that,
all Guy employees signed the following declaration:

Are you a member of a Trade Union?
What Union (if any)?
''I agree, if engaged, to observe all the rules and regulations of Guy Motors Limited and
particularly those special rules relating to the avoidance of disputes, as follows:
''I agree not, under any circumstances, to cease work or go slow until the matter under
dispute has been reported in writing within 48 hours notice by the Works Committee to the
General Works Manager who the firm undertake will reply within 48 hours. Failing a

satisfactory reply, the matter, in writing, shall be referred to the Managing Director with 48 hours notice, who undertakes to reply within 48 hours. If the reply is unsatisfactory, the Committee can refer the matter to the Executive of the Trades Union, who will communicate with the Managing Director and, providing the answer received is not satisfactory, then, and not till then, will I down tools.''

Since 1926, there has not been a strike at Guy Motors Ltd.

1927 With the development of their body building section, Guy were able to cater for the operators of large capacity vans. This was one of the largest of its time.

1927 A Guy gas producer vehicle. These were placed in service by Crown Agents for the Colonies, Empire Cotton Growing Corporation, Australian Government, etc. In parts of the world remote from petrol supplies, there has always been a demand for a vehicle which could be independent so this inspired the production of the Guy gas producer lorry in 1927. The fuel used was charcoal, and the vehicle showed a saving of 94 per cent in fuel costs where 18 lb of charcoal would do the work of a gallon of petrol! The vehicle would also run on various types of waste combustible products and it is interesting to note that one well-known municipality operated a fleet of Guy trucks on sewer gas.

Perhaps the best-ever illustration of the gas producer vehicle's versatility was the case of the prospective Eastern buyer who wrote and enquired whether the outfit would run on camel dung. Back home in Wolverhampton, Guy Motors sent someone round to the local farm for some cow dung, which was brought back and dried in a furnace. It was tried out and, whilst a certain amount of power was lost due to the quality of the "fuel", it worked. The order was obtained.

Around 1933, the weight of a vehicle was often about the same as the load it was specified to carry, but improvements in design and the use of more expensive but lighter materials, resulted in greater efficiency and lower running costs. The first vehicle which incorporated these features was the 'Wolf' 2 tonner, which appeared in 1933 and was christened by the late Sir Malcolm Campbell. This was soon followed by the 'Vixen' 3-4 tonner and the 'Otter'. The design of the 'Otter' was in the nature of a triumph because although it was built to carry 6 tons, it weighed under $2^{1}/_{2}$ tons fully equipped. These models continued to be improved, but in 1936 their production was somewhat curtailed as the Company was requested by the Government to produce military vehicles. By 1938 it ceased altogether, the Company then concentrating exclusively on Government contracts.

In 1941, however, the wartime needs of civilian operators were so great that a new model known as the 'Vixant' was produced, at the Government's request, from the units of the military 'Ant', for supply to the holders of Ministry of Transport Licences. This model was developed, and embodied many improvements made possible by experience with the 'Ant' on active service.

The end of the war saw the re-appearance of the 'Vixen' as a 4 tonner. This model was based on the pre-war one but with considerable improvements, and in 1946 there appeared the new 'Vixen' which included many new features evolved as the result of war-time experiences in many parts of the world and under widely varying conditions. The same year also saw the arrival of the new 'Wolf' 2-3 tonner.

In 1948, the 'Otter' 5-6- tonner was once again in production. The advantages and economy of diesel power was more and more realised and in 1950, the post-war 'Otter' diesel made its debut. Employing the very latest refinements in commercial vehicle design, the trio of 'Wolf, 'Vixen' and 'Otter' models, all with left-hand steering available, rapidly earned a reputation at home and overseas for 'long life and lowest running costs'. In response to the national need for increased exports, the overseas market was given priority and these vehicles were soon operating in many countries abroad.

Although there had been many refinements and improvements to the 'Wolf', 'Vixen' and 'Otter' models their outward appearance was little changed until in 1952 when an all-steel cab was designed for the 'Otter'. This was a handsome, roomy cab, with the advantage of easy breakdown for repair and assembly overseas.

A short wheelbase tractor model of the 'Otter' was developed in 1953 for the British Road Services. This was fitted with the all-steel cab and orders were placed (including trucks) for nearly 400 vehicles. The 'Otter' tractor was subsequently made generally available at home and with left-hand steering for overseas.

1953 Guy Otter tractor model for British Road Services.

With the post-war markets firmly established in the 2—6 tonner class, the Company decided in 1954 to re-enter the heavy vehicle market with the 'Big Otter' and 'Invincible' ranges. This was not an entirely new venture because as far back as 1932, a six-wheeled goods vehicle had been produced plus, of course, the background experience of designing and manufacturing heavy passenger vehicles for nearly forty years. The 'Invincible' range included four-, six- and eight-wheelers (12, 20 and 24 tons gross) designed for the maximum legal gross loads in this country, but where regulations and conditions permitted this could be increased. A variety of frame lengths and axle ratios made this a most versatile range, including tipper and trailer models. The 'Big Otter' $7^1/2$ tonner, powered by a Meadows $5^1/2$ litre engine, utilized most of the features of the 'Otter' including the all-steel cab. Truck, tipper and tractor units are manufactured. Thus 1954, the fortieth year of the Company, heralded the most ambitious programme since the war with a range of goods vehicles from 2-24 tons, and passenger vehicles from 20-100 seating capacity in production.

In 1955/6 another new model was introduced in the form of a 14 ton gross weight goods vehicle. Designated 'Warrior', this model was diesel-powered and had a completely new style of cab, based on the rounded design of the all-steel 'Otter' cab. This also was offered for a variety of applications such as tippers, trucks, tankers and tractors.

1957 Otter MkIII with restyled grille.

More new models were introduced in 1957. These included the 'Otter' Mk. III with restyled grille and a choice of power units and the 'Formidable' which was a more powerful version of the 'Warrior' with a new cab featuring deep wrap-around windscreens.

1955–1956 Warrior 14 ton gross weight goods vehicle.

If Guy Motors caused interest during 1955-7, it was small compared with the amount aroused at the 1958 Commercial Vehicle Show where the 'Invincible' Mk. II and 'Warrior' Mk. II had arrived. More powerful than ever, they not only offered a versatile range with a choice of modern diesel engines but they featured the most outstanding cab design ever to be seen on British Commercial vehicles. Angular, yet elegant, the forward leaning cab with a 'continental' look, had panoramic windscreens, spacious accommodation with luxurious seating, and offered such refinements as electric shaver, radio, cigarette lighter and was sound and heat insulated. This cab earned the praise of several authorities, including the Minister of Transport.

Guy Warrior MkII.

At the Commercial Vehicle Show at Earls Court in 1960, a 'Warrior' Mk. II tractor unit was exhibited with a new style of cab, featuring doors hinged at the front end which, when opened, revealed steps facilitating ease of entry. One of these cabs was fitted on a 'Warrior' with experimental air suspension on the rear axle for Tate & Lyle Ltd. Minor detail alterations appeared on the 'Invincible' Mk. II such as larger rectangular driving mirrors and a restyled double bumper arrangement.

Although 1961 saw nothing new in vehicle development, this year was to prove an important link in the chain of progression. In October, Jaguar Cars Ltd. acquired the business

Sir William Lyons

and physical assets of Guy Motors Ltd. Sir William Lyons had already entered the passenger vehicle field with the acquisition of Daimler and this latest move strengthened this interest and added commercial vehicles to the range offered by the Jaguar group of companies. The entire Guy range continued to be produced, and developed under the new name Guy Motors (Europe) Ltd.

The factory at Wolverhampton.

In September 1964 the new Guy 'Big J' range of heavy goods vehicles was announced featuring the powerful and compact 9.6 litre Cummins V6 diesel engine, although alternative power units were made progressively available. A new style cab was also introduced.

Passenger Vehicles

The first Guy passenger vehicle was produced in 1914, and was built to operate a combined mail and passenger service between Achnasheen and Aultbea in the Highlands of Scotland, at that time an appalling route and one of the most strenuous in the British Isles.

Following World War I, in 1919, the charabanc arrived and in 1921, the gearbox governor was omitted. Equipped with a thirty seater bus body this chassis soon became firmly established, and earned high praise from many operators. Up to this time, all Guy vehicles had a double reduction geared back axle employing bevels and spur gears in pairs, and it is interesting to note that in later years there was a tendency to revert to that type.

1914 Guy mail car.

1919 Guy charabanc.

1921 Guy 30-seater bus.

Rio de Janeiro ordered 170 Guy
buses in 1926.

In 1922, the Guy 'Promenade' runabout appeared and was a popular feature at Bournemouth and other seaside resorts. The year 1923 saw the advent of the one-man operated bus, with patent emergency exit at the rear although this was, of course, long before this safety feature became a legal obligation. Up to 1924 it was general practice for manufacturers to adapt goods vehicle chassis for passenger work, but in this year the Company produced Britain's first dropped frame chassis. This development introduced the era of vehicles with one-step entry, and an early result was the placing of an order with the Company by Rio de Janeiro for 170 Guy buses.

By 1925 it was obvious that the growing population of towns would necessitate the use of larger capacity transport. The six-wheel principle which the Company had already successfully developed was adapted to the drop frame chassis, and the first six-wheel double-decker was delivered to Wolverhampton Corporation in 1926. In 1927, a fleet of these buses appeared on the streets of London, these being the first six-wheelers ever to be operated in the capital. The vehicles were so popular that the London Public Omnibus Co. was soon bought up by the London General Omnibus Co. (the forerunner of the London Transport Executive).

Meanwhile, the rapid improvements in petrol bus design hastened the decline of tramcars, and municipalities owning electricity undertakings found themselves faced with the problem of maintaining the demand for electricity. Guy Motors came to the rescue in 1926 by producing the world's first six-wheeled double-deck trolleybus. This vehicle had regenerative control, which fed power back into the line and provided electric braking. It was supplied to Wolverhampton Corporation and after eleven years' service, during which it covered over 500,000 miles, it was only withdrawn because the body was out of date.

In 1928 the Company pioneered the six-wheeled double-deck sleeper coach, with 31 seats which were convertible to bunks, which was placed in service between London and Manchester and had a body by Strachan. Landliners Ltd. introduced the service and it is on record that a passenger on this predecessor of today's motorway coach, during its inaugural run, felt sick in a berth on the lower deck so was transferred upstairs and was sick!

1928 Guy 6-wheeler double-deck sleeper coach.

The year 1930 saw the first electric trolleybus introduced into South Africa, this being a Guy six-wheeled double-decker. Orders were also received from India, Italy, Belgium, Japan and other countries.

1930 Guy trolley bus for export.

The trolleybus was more economical both in maintenance and in operating cost, particularly so with the Guy patented system which has a compound motor which gives automatic braking, together with simultaneous regeneration of current. By this method, a saving of up to thirty per cent of the current used, depending upon the type of route, is effected. A period of six years elapsed before any other manufacturer offered regenerative control, which later became general practice.

As we have told in the chapter on goods vehicles, the 'Wolf' and 'Vixen' chassis appeared in 1933 and modified versions of these were produced as 14, 20 and 24 seater buses respectively. The same year witnessed the introduction of the Guy 'Arab' chassis for single and double deck buses, this being the first bus chassis designed to accommodate the Gardner oil engine. But with the approach of war, production of this chassis ceased along with that of the goods vehicles.

A fleet of wartime Guy arabs.

During the first years of the war, the manufacture of buses had ceased altogether, and the severe losses suffered by the public transport services through enemy action created such a serious shortage of essential transport for war workers that, in 1941, Guy Motors Ltd. were asked by the Ministry of Supply to produce a war-time version of the 'Arab' double-decker. Large numbers of these buses were produced, giving satisfactory service in the hands of many of the most important operators in the country. These chassis were about twenty per cent heavier than those of pre-war manufacture, this being due to the restricted use of light metals, but in 1946 the situation improved and the Company were again able to employ light alloys and pre-war steels in producing the post-war model.

A single-deck version of the 'Arab' on a 17 ft. 6 in. wheelbase was also put into production during 1946. Both double- and single-deck models incorporated many improvements resulting from the experience gained from operating war-time models under most difficult conditions. One improvement was the constant-mesh gearbox and friction clutch and, as an alternative, the fluid flywheel with a Wilson preselective epicyclic gearbox. The last mentioned was not new to Guy Motors because, as far back as 1933, vehicles with this type of transmission were produced. It is interesting to record that Guy Motors were the first to install the Gardner engine in a bus on a production basis and for many years they consistently standardized that engine in their diesel vehicles.

With the increasing demand, particularly from overseas, for a more powerful engine than the 6LW Gardner, Guy Motors collaborated with Henry Meadows Ltd. to produce the 10.35 litre Meadows-Guy 6-cylinder engine. After exhaustive testing, it was then offered as an alternative.

1946 Arab single-decker in Holland.

Arab single-decker in Wolverhampton.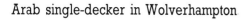

Arab single-decker in Burton-on-Trent.

Vixant 30-seater.

Arab double-decker in Ceylon.

Arab single-decker in Denmark.

Vixant coach in Holland.

Arab double-decker in Madrid.

In 1947, the 'Wolf' and 'Vixen' passenger vehicles were again in production and the building of bus bodies was started to ease the bottleneck in this direction, some being built under licence from Park Royal.

The next year saw the acquisition of the Sunbeam Trolleybus Co. Ltd. which created the largest trolleybus group in Britain. The success of this merger can be judged by the many repeat orders which came in from all over the world. The range consisted of the F4, a two-axled single- or double-deck chassis, the S7, a three-axled 30 ft. long double-deck model and the MF2B, a single-deck export chassis for transit-type bodies.

1954 Sunbeam 2-axle 30 ft long double-decker trolley bus – Walsall corporation.

A long wheelbase version of the 'Otter' designed for a 32 seater body, was produced in 1949 with either petrol or diesel power units available. There were a number of developments in 1950, the most important of which was probably the 'Arab' underfloor-engined single-decker. Another was the Mark IV 'Arab' with the new type fronted grille covering the radiator, this 'new look' being developed for the Birmingham Undertaking who subsequently took delivery of 300 chassis. A Mark IV 'Arab' was also produced as a single decker (18 ft. 5 in. wheelbase) to seat forty passengers. The fluid flywheel and epicyclic gearbox were available on the Mark IV 'Arab' chassis but many customers continued to specify the friction clutch and constant mesh gearbox. Several interesting models were developed in 1951, including an 'Arab' one-man operated underfloor-engined single-decker for Huddersfield Corporation, with a 43 seater body of Guy construction. Chassis of a similar type were also supplied to Southampton. Incidentally, a one-man operated vehicle was first produced by this Company way back in 1923. Another interesting model produced was an 'Arab' Mark III double-decker for the Central S.M.T. with a Guy-built low bridge body.

1951 Arab under-floor engined
one-man-operated single-deck –
Huddersfield corporation.

1948/1954 Otter diesel coach.

GUY

Arab under-floor engine bus in Rhodesia.

Arab single-decker in Lagos.
Operator J. N. Zarpas & Co. Limited.

Continually rising costs of passenger vehicle operation created a demand for a light-weight chassis, with the consequent saving in fuel consumption. The 'Arab' light-weight heavy duty underfloor-engined bus or coach chassis was produced in 1953 to effect this saving without sacrificing the robustness and accessibility which had always been a feature of Guy construction. Guy adaptability was very evident in the design and manufacture of an 'Arab' underfloor-engined three-axle model (the first made in this country) for the Rhodesian State Railways, this employing several unusual features including a third differential that could be locked by hand. A normal control version of the 'Vixen' 26 seater was designed in 1953 for the London Transport Executive with over eighty of this type being produced.

1953 Vixen 20-seater single-decker
– London transport.

1953 Arab 3-axle under-floor engined
bus – Rhodesian state railways.

So to 1954, with the Company in a strong position both at home and overseas. The policy of 'individually built for longest life and lowest running costs' proved to be sound time and time again. Guy passenger vehicles were then operated by over 150 undertakings in this country and 26 countries overseas. The associate, the Sunbeam Trolleybus Co. was still making trolleybus history – this time with the development of the first two-axle chassis with 30 ft. overall length.

1954 Arab lightweight heavy-duty under-floor engined coach.

In 1957, ten modified 'Arab' chassis were constructed for Johannesburg Municipal Transport, utilizing the three-axled layout and fitted with 12 litre Rolls-Royce diesel engines. The double-deck bodies were constructed by Bus Bodies S.A. Ltd. and these 'Johannesburg Giants' accommodated 105 passengers, probably making them the largest buses in the world at that time.

The year 1959 saw Guy making double-decker history when a double-decker with all-round air suspension and disc brakes was announced and christened the 'Wulfrunian'. It was primarily developed for the West Riding Automobile Co. who later ordered over ninety of these advanced design buses. Several other companies and municipal operators added 'Wulfrunian' buses to their fleets, giving Guy the distinction of being first in the field yet again.

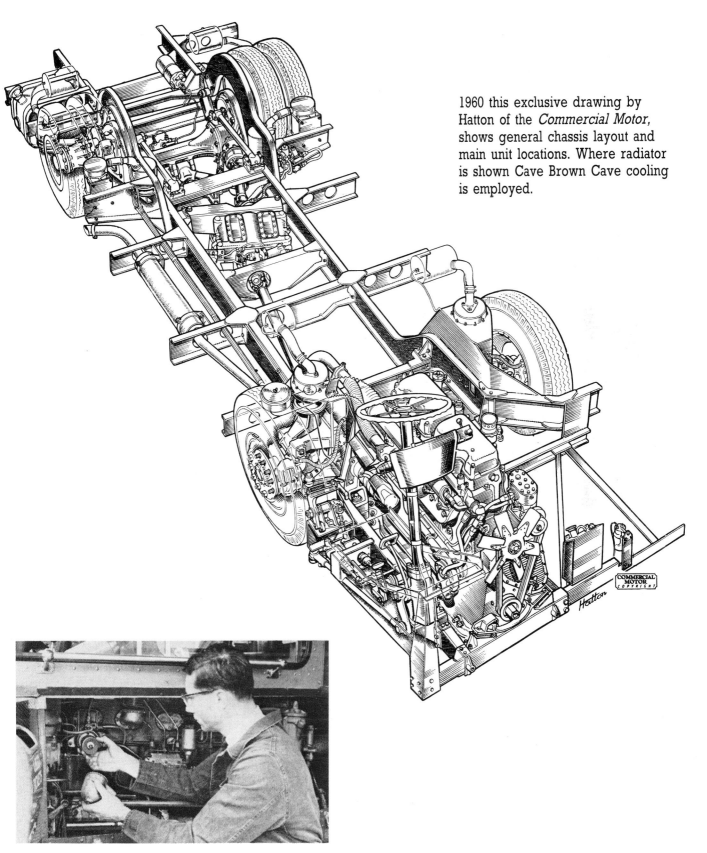

1960 this exclusive drawing by Hatton of the *Commercial Motor*, shows general chassis layout and main unit locations. Where radiator is shown Cave Brown Cave cooling is employed.

Senior apprentice Robin Hannay demonstrating engine access.

GUY

In 1960, a 'Victory' chassis with air suspension was supplied to a Netherlands operator for use as a single deck luxury coach. A feature of this was the ramped flooring, which raised the seating and enabled luggage to be stowed beneath the floor. The bodywork included kitchen and toilet compartments, with food being served *en route* by a hostess. This body design was the forerunner of present day luxury coach body design. Another interesting passenger vehicle supplied during the year was a double-deck 'Arab' with forward entrance and 'half-front' built for Chester Corporation who subsequently ordered more.

1960 Guy Victory export bus fitted with air suspension supplied to Netherlands operator with raised seating and luggage storage underneath.

Further orders were also received for the 'Wulfrunian' double-decker from the transport departments of Wolverhampton Corporation, Bury Corporation and West Wales Motors Ltd. 'Victory' passenger chassis were further developed specifically for the export markets, and proved both very popular and highly successful.

Wulfrunian entering Queen's Square, Wolverhampton.

Military Vehicles

The first vehicles of this type were built in 1923 under a Government subsidy, and had pneumatic tyres. By 1924, however, the Company was producing vehicles with caterpillar tracks in place of rear wheels, whilst retaining the ordinary wheels on the front. These vehicles were supplied to the Admiralty, the War Office and the Crown Agents for the Colonies. The caterpillar tracks provided considerably increased ground adhesion, but were short-lived owing to mud and grit causing excessive wear on the track joints.

1923 Guy military general service
vehicle fitted with pneumatic tyres.

1924 one of the earliest "roadless"
vehicles.

 **GUY**

1928 Guy 6-wheeled
armoured car – Indian Government.

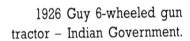

1926 Guy 6-wheeled gun
tractor – Indian Government.

1928 Guy 6-wheeled armoured
car chassis on test.

1931 Guy 8-wheel drive.

1938 Guy army GS wagon.

Meanwhile experiments were going on with a rigid six-wheeler and in 1926 the first British vehicle of this type was produced. This model had four rear-driving wheels mounted on a rocking cross-shaft, forming a bogie which allowed a large measure of articulation. This advantage was consolidated by the use of overall chains for duty in the most difficult traction conditions, with great success. The Guy six-wheeler has been supplied as an Army G.S. wagon, artillery tractor, field workshop and searchlight generator vehicle, and many armoured cars were built on this chassis for the India Office in 1928. In stages of logical development followed the six-wheel and eight-wheel driven vehicles, placed in service in 1931. The eight-wheel driven type would go literally anywhere if four of its eight wheels could get a grip and would negotiate a trench six feet wide without dropping into it.

In 1936, the Company was requested by the Government to produce a four-wheeled military truck to a War Department specification and to incorporate, if possible, all major units, such as engines, axles and steering gear used for commercial vehicles. The specificaton called for high ground clearance, short wheelbase, small turning circle, exceptionally good forward position for the driver and large section low pressure tyres. In due course, a vehicle designated the 'Ant' was born and after exhaustive military trials, was approved and ordered in large quantities.

Further requests by the War Department resulted in the production in 1938 of the 'Quad-Ant' and 'Lizard'. Both were four-wheeled (all driven) tractor vehicles and, in passing their military tests, proved capable of hauling gross loads of six to fourteen tons up gradients of 1 in 2. In "Drive for Freedom" by Charles Graves, these vehicles are referred to as being "among the more satisfactory items of equipment which the British Expeditionary Force took to France in 1939". In connection with military requirements, the Company had manufactured for many years two types of mobile searchlight units, a six-wheeled type with belt-driven generator and a four-wheeled type with the engine directly coupled to the generator, driving through the armature to the gearbox, but supplying current to the searchlight only when the vehicle was stationary and out of gear. The introduction of radar stopped production of these vehicles, although at the time this was not known.

As a development of the four-wheel drive Guy 'Quad-Ant' the Company produced the first British rear-engined four-wheel drive armoured car. It was suggested to the War Office that the hull and turret of bullet proof homogenous hard unmachinable plate should be of welded instead of riveted construction but the Government Technical Department advised it was not commercially possible to weld this material. Undaunted, the Company offered to weld the first batch, and if unsuccessful to stand the cost. After a few months, the 'impossible' was accomplished and welded construction became general practice. One advantage of welded construction was the very considerable reduction in the number of casualties resulting from 'splash' and rivet heads flying around inside the tanks while a second was a reduction in the price of the material per tank by elimination of the machining of the plate, saving the country some £100,000,000 on tank production. Finally, the vehicle, being waterproof, was able to "wade" to a considerable depth.

Guy armoured cars on desert patrol during the war.

The Company placed their patents and methods on this important development at the free disposal of the Government in the national interest, for the duration of the war. This was gratefully acknowledged and an Award was made to the Company by the Royal Commission on Awards to Inventors for the original pre-war idea of welding bullet proof homogeneous hard armour plate on armoured fighting vehicles.

One of the difficulties created by the war was the shortage of manpower, coupled with the necessity for increased production of military vehicles. In solving this problem, the Company introduced a scheme whereby senior pupils and masters from local schools were given the opportunity of doing war work during their holidays. They were employed on the assembly of jigs for the bodies for army trucks, and so great was the response that a separate department was set up and excellent work was produced. When the boys returned to school, the scheme was continued by the employment, as part-time workers, of women during the day and business and professional men in the evenings. One of the first and most enthusiastic volunteers was a County Court Judge, who served for nearly four years and was largely responsible for the success of the project.

In those early days of the war, most part-time workers had not previously been eligible for unemployment insurance and declined to be employed through the Labour Exchange but, in view of the national emergency, were engaged without this formality. This action brought a threat from the Ministry of Labour to prosecute Mr. Guy, but fortunately the law was amended before this happened.

The first advertisement for part-time workers resulted in over 1,000 applications, and reproduced here is a poster which was symbolic of the scheme. An interesting booklet was published entitled ''The Family goes to War'' and the following extract from this is worthy of recording:

"A Tribute to Part-Time Workers"

'Full and part-time workers, sharing the reflected glory of their fighting brothers have good cause to feel proud of their efforts . . . You, in a war job, think of yourself as part of that army that is fighting its way to Final Victory, to a Victory that must surely crown your joint efforts. We pay tribute to you, who after a hard day's toil at the benches, serve in a hospital during your leisure hours . . .

To you, the girl who, on learning the tragic loss of your nearest and dearest on active service, fights back through a job making munitions . . . To you, who find no handicap in age, but volunteer in the evening of your life to resume where you left off twenty-five years ago . . . To those of you who volunteered for a three-day shift, but, in order to increase output, now work for six . . . You and you and you who, when the day is done in the factory, bravely face your domestic problems . . . You, whose daily sacrifice helps to supply the sinews of war for the husbands and brothers who are fighting their way home to you . . . To you all we say this: ''When you are feeling tired, don't be discouraged, if you do, don't give up''. . . remember this, our Fighting Forces are depending on you; without your help they face a losing battle. Don't let them down''.

Engine design and development

During World War I, two types of radial aero-engines were produced. The first was the 7-cylinder 'Wasp' in 1917, this being followed in 1918 by the 9-cylinder 'Dragonfly'. In the production of the latter, the Company can claim an engineering achievement, as this 350 hp engine was produced from initial design to complete unit in only 24 days. This year also saw the arrival of a 12 cylinder aero-engine.

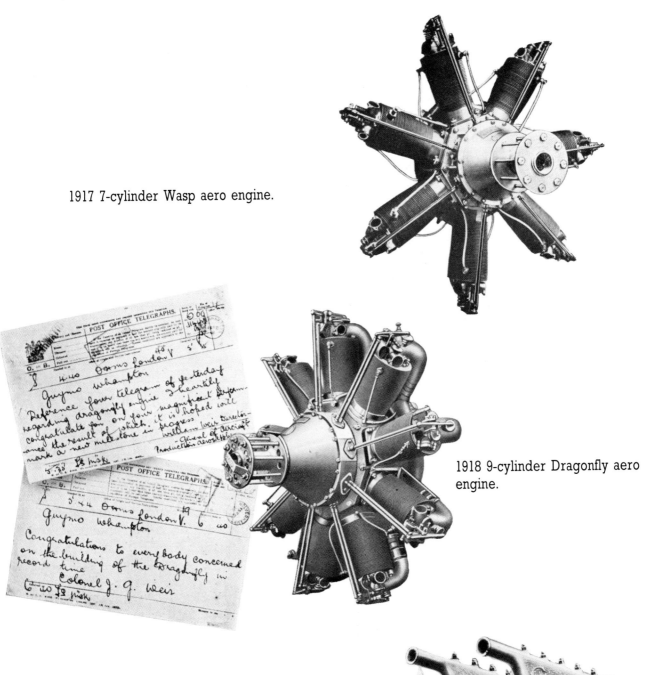

1917 7-cylinder Wasp aero engine.

1918 9-cylinder Dragonfly aero engine.

1918 8-cylinder engine with inclined valves and heads.

1918 accessibility of the engine.

The versatility of the Company's designers is readily shown by the various engine types produced. Soon after World War I, Guy vehicles were fitted with a unique type of engine which was a distinct advance over all other makes at that time. Whereas other commercial vehicle engines had side valves and fixed heads, Guy incorporated inclined valves and inclined detachable heads. Apart from accessibility, the design of the combustion chamber was such that the efficiency of the engine was at least equal to that of any contemporary overhead valve type.

Service

The requirements of road transport operators vary considerably and deviations from standard are often incorporated in fleets of vehicles to meet customer's requirements. The problem of service is one of the greatest. The Service Department at the factory at Wolverhampton contained stores in which there were over 45,000 bins, in which stocks of more than 125,000 different parts were regularly carried. These parts ranged from gaskets to complete components for vehicles produced during the previous 25 years. In addition, large stocks of spare parts were carried at the London Depot and by Guy agents throughout the world.

A view of the 45,000 bins in the spare parts stores.

Service department stores

Engine reconditioning

Axle reconditioning

Part of the fitting shop.

The Company had a standing instruction that it was more important to supply a part required to keep a Guy vehicle on the road than to produce a new one. Consequently, a reputation was built up for unparalleled service.

In the factory

Careful production ensures 'longer life and lower running costs'. Guy production methods, as well as the testing to which every vehicle was subjected, were most comprehensive. Raw materials went through laboratory tests before being passed for production, and inspectors scrutinised every part during manufacture. The extensive shops were laid out efficiently to handle the construction of every type of commercial and passenger vehicle, and the standard of workmanship was extremely high.

On completion every chassis was fully laden and taken out three times for separate road tests by different drivers, for at least a thirty mile road run. Each tester had to complete a detailed report on every aspect of the new vehicle, including final tuning and adjustments.

During World War II, a complete electricity generating station was installed, thus making the factory self-supporting and immune from frequent power cuts.

The drawing office.

The gunshop

Guy Motors did their share towards the defence programme during World War II, and what better testimony could there be than the fact that the craftsmanship was equal to the very high standard demanded for such contracts.

Rio de Janeiro Guys in service 10 years after the petrol engines were changed to diesels.

Welfare

The Company always realised its responsibility for the welfare of its employees, and there was an excellent welfare club run by a committee of the workpeople. An extensive sports ground adjoined the factory with cricket and football pitches, tennis courts and a bowling green. In the centre of this sports ground the canteen, with the most modern kitchen equipment of the time, provided up to 500 main meals a day while also being used for concerts, whist drives, dances and table tennis. Families of the employees were not forgotten, and the children were given outings every summer and a party at Christmas. In 1936, the Company was one of the first to voluntarily initiate holidays with pay for all workers.

Long service certificates were awarded to employees with twenty years service and by 1954, 293 employees had received certificates with 62 of these having over thirty years service to their credit.

During World War II, continuous employment under blackout conditions began to affect the health of the employees, and this led to the introduction of sun-ray equipment in the works clinic. Here trained nurses were in constant attendance to deal with cases of accident or illness, and a doctor made regular visits. All employees, subject to the doctor's approval, were encouraged to take a course of sun-ray free of charge in the Company's time, the tonic effect of this treatment undoubtedly reducing the amount of time lost through fatigue and illness.

Works canteen.

Group of presentations made in 1944 for twenty years' service.

The garden in memory of the fallen in both world wars.

Transport through the syzygies

As the scope of wartime advertising was very properly restricted, and as orders could not be accepted for the Company's commercial models, it was felt that our publicity must be used to keep our name before the public, so that it should be remembered in association with transport in post-war years.

Influenced and impressed by the widespread interest shown in crossword puzzles, in the questions submitted to the Brains Trust and in the enthusiasm evoked by Spelling Bees and in other means of relief from the problems of war, it was decided that the advertisements should aim at arousing educational and historical interest. Hence "Transport through the Syzygies".

1919 Guy 8-cylinder car.

1919 automatic lubrication system.

FRONT DUMB IRON SHACKLE.
FRONT SUSPENSION BALL PIN

FRONT SPRING SHACKLE.

OVERFLOW TO CRANKCASE.

STEERING BOX.

PUMP OPERATED BY EXTREME STEERING LOCK.

PEDAL SHAFT BRACKET.

SUBFRAME SUSPENSION BALL.
SUSPENSION LINK.

BRAKE CROSS SHAFT.

REAR SPRING SHACKLE.

The 13/36 hp Touring Car.

GUY

The Guy 20 hp V8 5-seater Tourer, with Mr Sydney S. Guy at the wheel. This is the prototype. Later models had a deeper header tank on the radiator.

1914 30 cwt vehicle.

1914 3-point suspended sub-frame.

1920 the first roadless farmers vehicle.

In use in New Zealand for over 25 years, this 2/3 tonner had pneumatics on the rear and still the original solid tyres on the front.

The Guy 30 cwt lorry and engine.

1922 articulated 6-wheeler.

1922 2^1/$_2$/3 ton electric battery vehicle.

1923 road-rail vehicle.

1923 road-rail vehicle engine.

The 1923 road-rail vehicles leaving the factory.

1920 2^1/$_2$ ton Guy shown at first post-war commercial vehicle show for Peek Freans.

A well-loaded Guy wagon on early 1920s.

Another "first" was the military
vehicle produced in 1923 with
pneumatic tyres.

1920 the first roadless farmer
vehicle – a Guy.

Cross-country trial for caterpillar
Guy for the War Office.

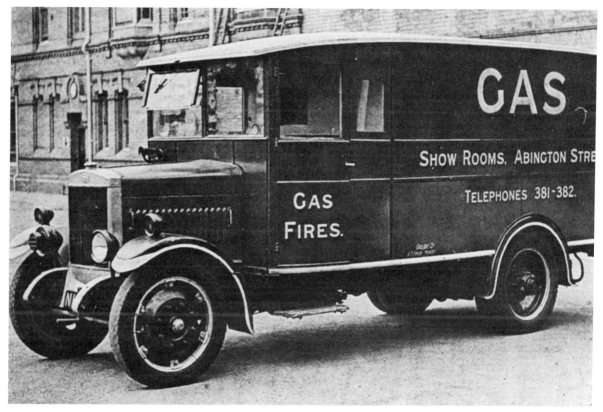

A Guy OND-type chassis with van body.

1927 Guy gas-producer chassis and a complete vehicle.

Nuneaton, Guy Fire Engine.

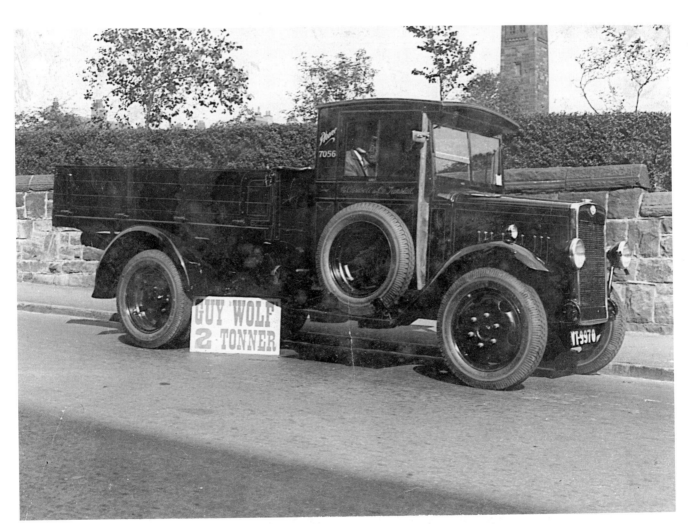

Guy Wolf 2 tonner.

The late Sir Malcolm Campbell, christening the new Guy "Wolf" May 1933.

A Guy 2 ton van introduced in 1923.

Wolf 2 tonners for J. Lyons and Co. Limited.

1934 Wolf for Pilkington Brothers Limited.

1935 Wolf vans, Electricity Supply Department.

1934 Wolf lorry.

1934 Otter 6 tonner.

1935 Parcel delivery van.

1939 Guy 6 ton Otter for Firth and Brown.

1941 war time Vixants.

1941/1945 a Vixant produced for civilian operators during the war from the miliary Ant version.

1947 Wolf 2/3 ton Chiver's Jellies van.

1947 Wolf 2/3 tonner.

1947 Vixant 4 tonner.

1947 Vixant travelling shop.

1947 Wolf 2/3 tonner drop-side lorry.

1947 Vixant 4 tonner pantechnicon.

1947 Vixant travelling milk bar.

1947 Vixant 4 tonner in Demark.

1947 Vixant refrigerator van.

1948 5/6 ton Otter goods vehicle.

1948 Vixant 4 tonner.

Vixant 4 tonner for
John Lewis Partnership.

Otter tractor unit in Kenya.

1954 6 tonner refuge carrier in Nigeria.

Otter tipper in Norway.

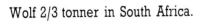

Wolf 2/3 tonner in South Africa.

Wolf diesel for Lewis's.

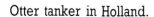

Otter tanker in Holland.

Vixant and trailer in Holland.

1950 Guy Otter diesel goods vehicle.

Otter 6 tonner van.

Wolf diesel 2/3 ton for Wallis and Co.

1955 Otter coal truck.

1954 Otter 6 tonner for Hill's.

1954 Invincible 6-wheeler.

1954 Invincible 4-wheeler.

1954 Big Otter 7^{1}/$_{2}$ tonner.

1954 Invincible 8-wheeler tanker.

Otter MkIII pantechnicon.

1957 Guy Formidable tractor unit with P. G. Walton.

Warrior 8-wheel articulated outfit with Safeway Limited.

Latest version Otter with
Silent Night Limited.

(Above and right) Guy Warrior tippers.

Guy Invincible tipper.

GUY

Guy Warrior milk tanker.

Guy Warrior petrol tanker.

78

Guy Warrior lwb 4-wheeler bulk carrier.

Guy Warrior 6-wheeler

Bonneted version of Invincible
tractor in South Africa.

Guy Invincible MkII, IV,
6- and 8-wheelers.

Guys at 1962 Commercial Vehicle Show, one with special cab for Tate and Lyle.

8-wheeler Invincible with Regent Oil.

September 1964 sees introduction of big J range, with new style cabs and 9.6 litre commins V6 diesel engines.

Guy 23-seater charabanc, note passenger to right of driver.

Early assembly bays at Guys Motors Limited.

An early pay-as-you-enter bus on a Guy 30 cwt chassis in 1920.

1921 30-seater Guy bus.

Typical promenade "toastrack" Guy run-about from mid-1920s.

Guy OND-chassis with 14-seat body, new in August 1926.

Guy charabanc in mid-1920s at Great Orme Head, North Wales.

1923 one-man-operated Guy bus.

Britain's first low-loader drop-frame
chassis – a 1924 Guy.

Aveling and Porter roadroller, being overtaken by a Guy single-decker!

1926 Britain's first 6-wheeler double-deck Guy bus operated by Wolverhampton corporation.

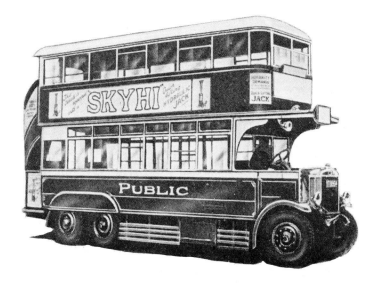

1927 Guy 6-wheeler double-deck bus with London Omnibus Company.

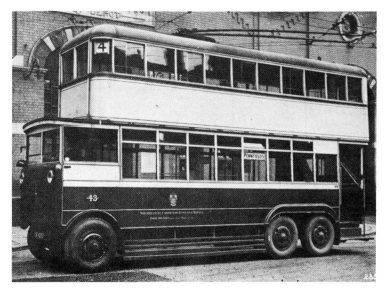

1929 Guy trolley bus and chassis. Note unusual position of motor.

32-seater Guy single deck bus.

1927 B-type chassis with 21-seat body.

1927 BB type with 31-seat dual entrance bodywork.

1929 Guy Fox 6-wheel bus chassis with petrol engine.

1929 Guy CX 60-seat double-deck in service in Leicester.

Two Guy FBB buses exported to
China in 1929.

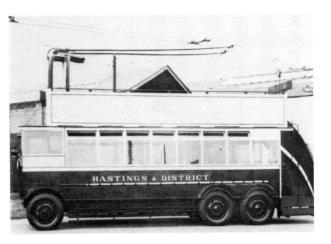

Hastings double-deck open top Guy trolley bus.

1930 Guy 6-wheeler trolley bus in Cape Town.

1930 Guy single-deck trolley bus for Japan.

1933 Guy arabs fitted with Gardner diesel engines.

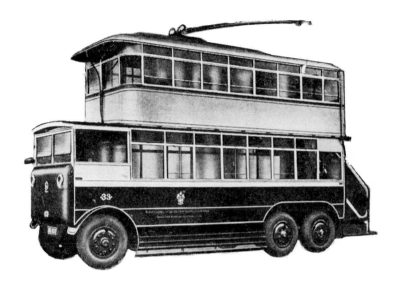

World's first 6-wheeler pneumatic tyred double-deck trolley bus. It covered 500,000 miles in 11 years' service.

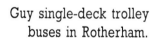

Guy single-deck trolley buses in Rotherham.

Guy trolley bus double-deck in Llanelli.

1930 first trolley bus in South Africa.

1930 Guy trolley bus being loaded aboard ship for overseas service.

A Guy Wolf in Delhi.

A Guy Wolf 20-seater.

Fleets of Guys in Southampton.

 GUY

A fleet of Guy trolley buses in Newcastle.

A Guy bus in Belfast.

Latest Guy trolley bus chassis.

BT trolley buses with Roe bodies in 1937 at Wolverhampton.

Guy Arab with Gardner oil engine in Wolverhampton.

GUY

1933 Leeds city transport took delivery of six Arabs with Gardner engines.

A typical wartime arab MkII, with Charles H. Roe utility low bridge body.

Arab single-decker with Guy body in Scotland.

Vixant 30 seater in Holland.

Arab single-decker in Nyasaland.

1948 Sunbeam trolley bus supplied to Walsall corporation. The acquisition of the Sunbeam Trolley Bus Company Limited created the largest British trolley bus group.

1948 Arab MkIV double-decker – Birmingham corporation (1 of 300 supplied).

Arab under-floor engined coach in Portugal – operator Capristanos.

Arab under-floor engined coach in Holland – operator Brabena.

1954 Arab double-decker –
Benbrough corporation.

Arab under-floor engined bus in South Africa – Pietermaritzburg corporation.

Otter diesel light coach – Punjab state transport.

1957 ten of these modified Arabs were supplied to Johannesburg Municipal transport. They have 12 litre Rolls-Royce engines and bodies built by Bus Bodies (S.A.) Limited, accommodate 105 passengers.

1959 one of a number of Guy Seals sold in Portugal. This 24-seat coach has a body built in that country.

1959 Guy Wulfrunian was announced in this year. Fitted with all-round air suspension and disc brakes, it was truly in advance of its time.

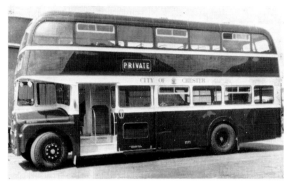

1960 Arab MkV supplied to Chester Corporation with forward entrance and "half front" design.

Guy Arab MkV with Strachan double-deck body at the 1962 Commercial Show.

GUY

Coats of arms of some British and some overseas operators of Guy buses.

SOME OVERSEAS OPERATORS OF GUY "ARAB" BUSES

BULAWAYO · LAHORE · TENERIFE · CAPETOWN

BERGEN DENMARK · JOHANNESBURG · LYNGBY DENMARK

PERTH WESTERN AUSTRALIA · SALISBURY Sthn. RHODESIA

COLOMBO · MADRID · LAS PALMAS · DURBAN · KHARTOUM

NUMBER ONE

SOME BRITISH OPERATORS OF GUY "ARAB" BUSES

BIRMINGHAM

LANCASTER

MAIDSTONE

LUTON

GRIMSBY

LIVERPOOL

CHESTER

NOTTINGHAM

BRADFORD

DERBY

NEWPORT

GUY ARAB   BIRMINGHAM

NEWCASTLE upon TYNE

LEIGH

STOCKPORT

WOLVERHAMPTON

SHEFFIELD

ACCRINGTON

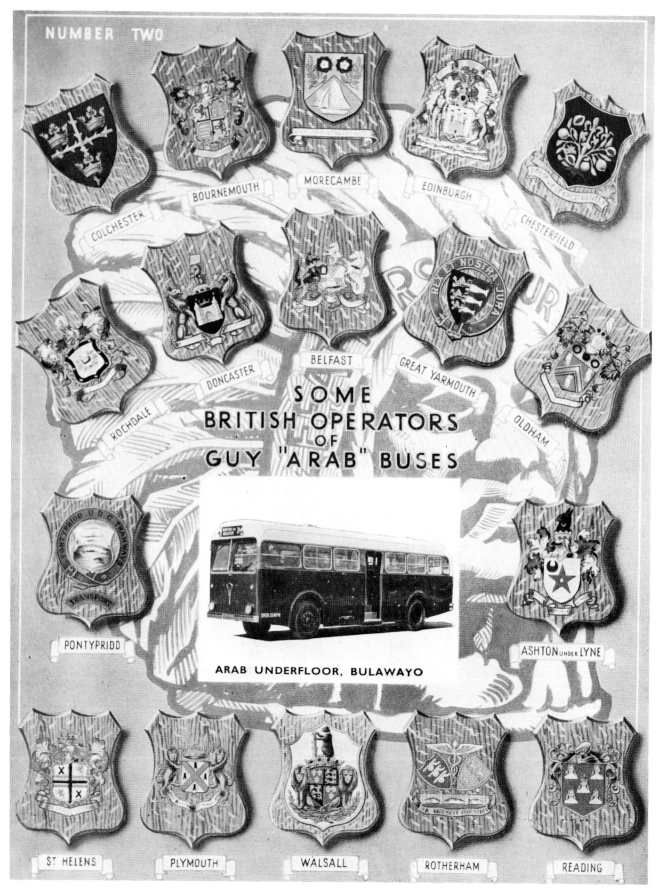

NUMBER TWO

COLCHESTER · BOURNEMOUTH · MORECAMBE · EDINBURGH · CHESTERFIELD

ROCHDALE · DONCASTER · BELFAST · GREAT YARMOUTH · OLDHAM

SOME
BRITISH OPERATORS
OF
GUY "ARAB" BUSES

PONTYPRIDD

ARAB UNDERFLOOR, BULAWAYO

ASHTON UNDER LYNE

ST. HELENS · PLYMOUTH · WALSALL · ROTHERHAM · READING

NUMBER THREE

SOME
BRITISH OPERATORS
OF
GUY "ARAB" BUSES

GUY ARAB, WALSALL

MIDDLESBROUGH
HASLINGDEN
LINCOLN
BURTON on TRENT
WEST BROMWICH
CARDIFF
STOCKTON
BURNLEY
SWINDON
SOUTHAMPTON
SUNDERLAND
BARROW in FURNESS
SOUTH SHIELDS
WEST HARTLEPOOL
BIRKENHEAD
LEEDS
GLASGOW

1938 army 6-wheeled search light generator chassis.

1938 the first British rear engine four-wheel drive all-welded armoured car.

1940 Guy Quadant four-wheel drive GS wagon.

1939 Quadant gun tractor in France
during the first winter of the war.

1924 Admiralty roadless fleet of Guys.

1926 a Guy 6-wheeler on very rough ground.

1926 a large fleet of Guy 6-wheeled type vehicles in use with the Army.

1927

1927 Guy 6-wheelers with and without caterpillar tracks.

1927 6-wheeled gun tractor in India.

1927 Guy 6-wheeler used for tsetse fly
extermination by cutting and burning.

1928 armoured car chassis
under test under full load.

1928 the complete armoured car.

1931 Guy 6-wheel drive.

GUY

1931 Guy 8-wheel drive on test.

1937 Guy Ant air compressor vehicle.

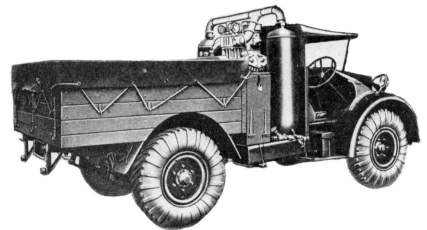

1938 Guy Lizard four-wheel drive cross country type.

1938 Guy Quadant four-wheel
drive military vehicle.

1938 part of a large fleet of
Guy Ants for military work.

1938 rear view of Guy four-wheel
drive armoured car.

1939 a view of the armoured car body welding department.

1939 the Guy search light generator lorry.

Special armoured command post vehicle believed used by Field Marshal Montgomery.

The late Judge Caporn and school boys at work in the body shop during their holidays.

A reproduction of the poster which helped to publicise the scheme.

Sections of the service stores –
engine reconditioning – rear axle
and gearbox unit assembly.

A view of the London Depot.

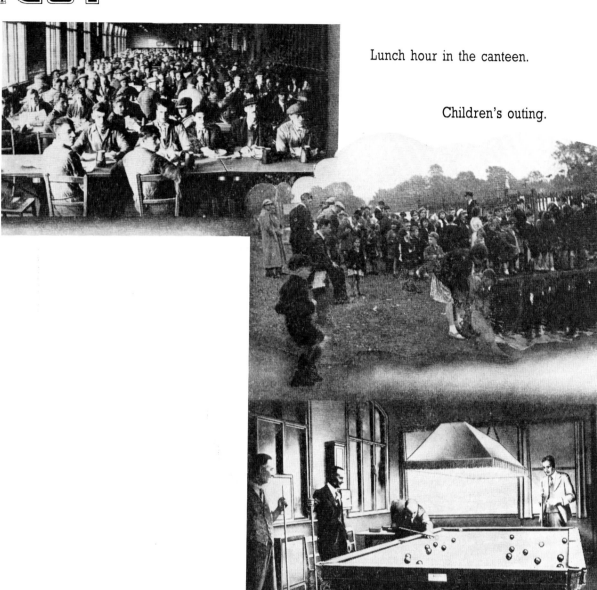

Lunch hour in the canteen.

Children's outing.

In the billiard room.

The annual staff dance.

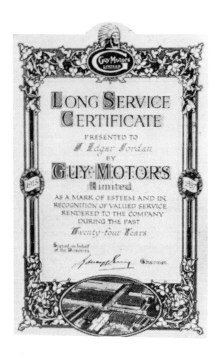

24 year long service certificate
presentation – bowling club –
bowling green – tennis courts –
ladies' hockey club.

**GUY**

Cricket match in progress.

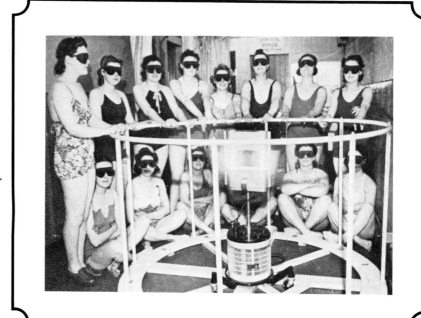

Sun-ray treatment.

The gun shop. Anti-aircraft gun reconditioning.

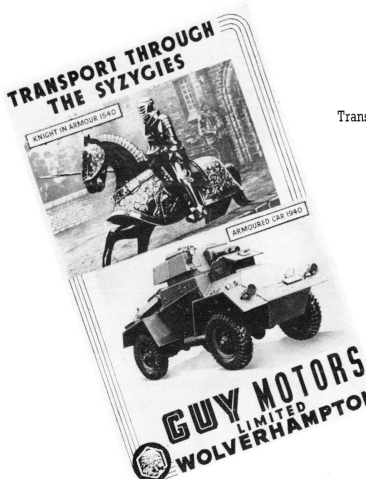

Transport through the Syzygies advertising.

GUY

TRANSPORT THROUGH THE SYZYGIES

STEAM CARRIAGE 1827

GUY BUS 1944

GUY MOTOR
LIMITED
WOLVERHAMPTON

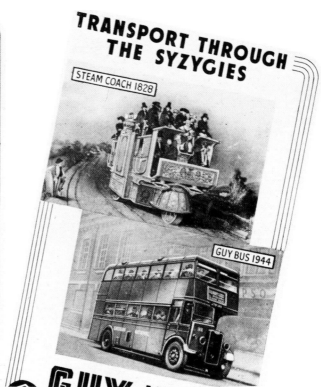
TRANSPORT THROUGH THE SYZYGIES

STEAM COACH 1828

GUY BUS 1944

GUY

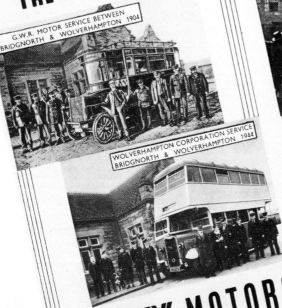
TRANSPORT THROUGH THE SYZYGIES

G.W.R. MOTOR SERVICE BETWEEN
BRIDGNORTH & WOLVERHAMPTON 1904

WOLVERHAMPTON CORPORATION SERVICE
BRIDGNORTH & WOLVERHAMPTON 1944

GUY MOTORS
LIMITED
WOLVERHAMPTON

TRANSPORT THROUGH
THE SYZYGIES

ENGLAND 1843

ENGLAND 1943

GUY MOTORS
LIMITED
WOLVERHAMPTON

The author's preserved 1935 Guy
Wolf 20-seater single-deck
ex-Llandudno.

Preserved Guy 6-wheeled trolley bus.

EARLY GUY DIRECTORS

T. STUDDY HOOPER
1914-1921

The late SAMUEL BAYLISS
1914-1915

The late J. A. JORDAN
1914-1931

The late SIR FRANCIS PEPPER
1921-1931

The late A. E. OWEN
1923-1929

J. H. BEAN, C.B.E.
1927-1931

The late G. H. SUMNER SMITH
1932-1934

A. E. WEBB
1932-1935

W. EWART GUY
Present Director

W. OSWALD PERRY
Present Director

W. E. BULLOCK
Present Director